Mary Chapin Carpenter

A Place in the World

Management: Borman Entertainment
Piano/Vocal Arrangements by John Nicholas
Photography by Caroline Greyshock

Mary Chapin Carpenter

A *Place In The World* is the sixth collection of songs I've come up with since I began making records in 1987. Some days it's as if the past ten years have just hurtled by, other days I seem to relive, not only each year, but every day and every moment that has made up those days, in slow motion.

Yet, to forget that each perspective is necessary is to lose sight of the most valuable lesson of creativity: the darker experiences and feelings can be as much the markers of humanity as the more uplifting moments, and that our humanity is what compels us to create, to express, to communicate.

The late Bill Monroe declared that his songs did not really "belong" to him in the conventional way we think of writers claiming ownership of their work; rather, he felt that songs were always kind of floating above him and every once in a while he would get to reach up and pull one down. Iris Dement, on the other hand, describes the process of writing as akin to "waiting" for songs to arrive, and her records as evidence of their "glorious visits."

I think Iris and Mr. Monroe have captured what is mystical and mysterious about creativity. What's obvious here is that every writer has their own way of thinking about how their songs come forth. The way they feel about it . . . keenly . . . passionately . . . reverently . . . is as important as the songs themselves.

Sometimes I think songs are like musical postcards that arrive from some unknown place, or snapshots that capture who and where you are at critical times. And when I don't have a clue where they've come from, it does seem less important to wonder about their origins than it does just to be glad they got here.

And now, *A Place In The World* makes me glad—after ten years, a million zillion miles, a couple of love affairs, a bunch of mistakes, a few victories, some dark days and some brilliant nights. This is, after all, what it's about.

Mary Chapin Carpenter

January 1997

A PLACE IN THE WORLD

CONTENTS

Keeping The Faith

Words and Music by Mary Chapin Carpenter

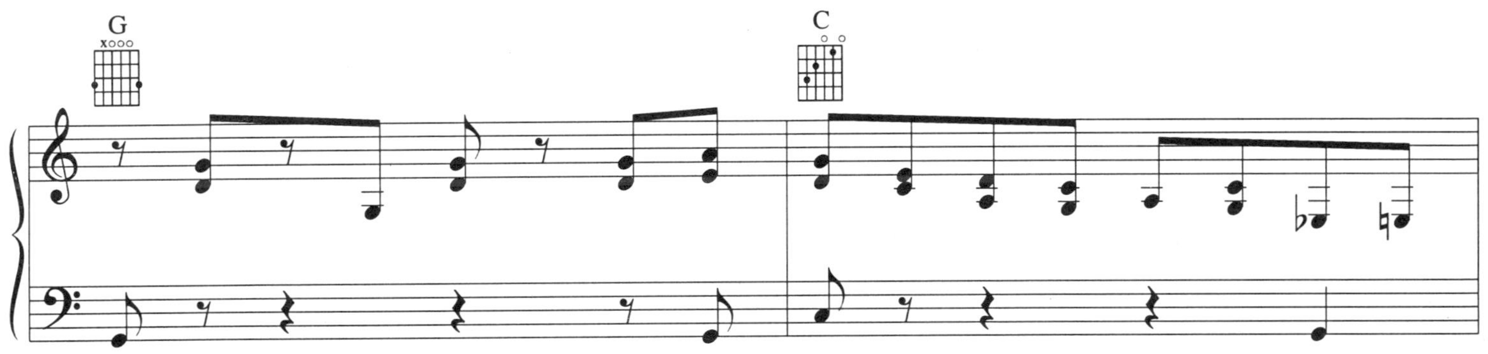

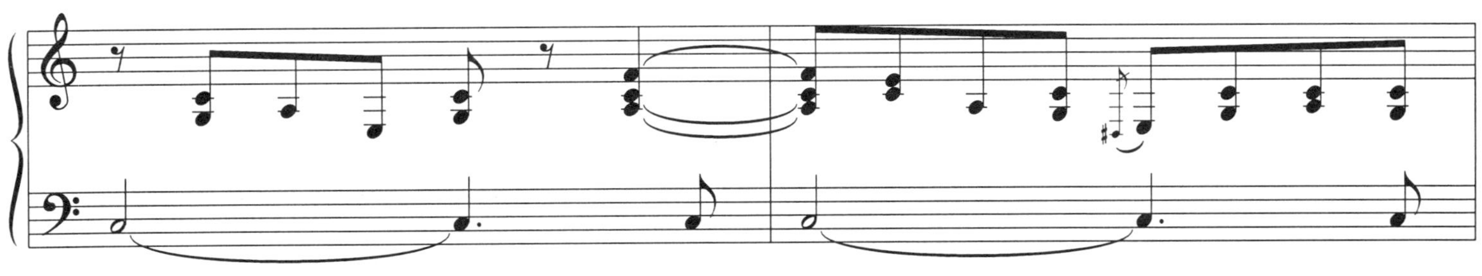

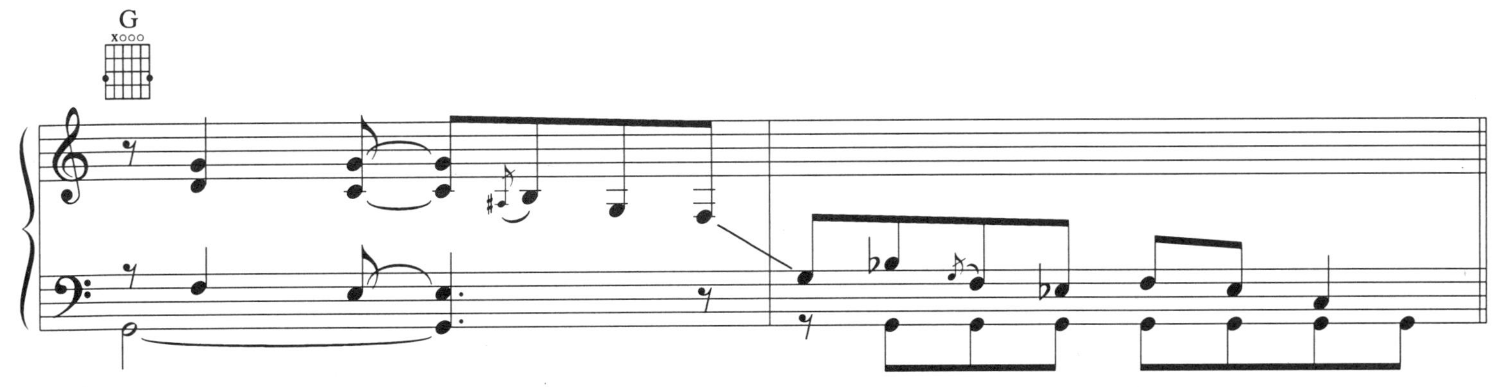

C
When it's been that kind of day, ba - by,
When your head's not mak - ing sense, ba - by,
It's the wea - ry, it's the lone - some,

G
C
when ev - 'ry - thing is not what it should be,
when your heart is just a mys - ter - y,
it's the for - est that we just can't see.

ev - 'ry - bod - y's had their say, let's
when you're sit - ting on the fence in -
Don't for - get now, there ain't no one who

G
C
just say the day is his - to - ry, and keep
stead of know - ing where you're sup - posed to be, well, just keep
is - n't try - ing to see be - yond the trees. So just keep
F
G
C
F
keep - ing the faith,
keep - ing the faith
To Coda
G
C
F
G
C
ev - 'ry day.
1. We're
2.3. We'll be
keep - ing the faith.
Keep

1.
F
G
C
keep - ing the faith. Don't give it a - way.
2.
F
G
C
F
keep - ing the faith. Don't get in the way - ee - ay.
G
C
F
G
C

F
G
C
F
G
C
F
G
F
All the style, all the mon - ey, all the pow - er you
G
C
F
G
can buy, won't do noth - ing if there's some - thing
Am
G
D.S. al Coda
miss - ing way down deep in - side.

Coda
F
G
C
keep - ing the faith. Don't
give it a - way - ee - ay.
F
G
C
F
G
Am
Keep - ing the faith
ev - 'ry day. We'll be
F
G
C
keep - ing the faith.
Oh,

F
G
C
keep - ing the faith. Don't give it a - way.
F
G
C
F
G
C
F
G
C
F
G
C

Hero In Your Own Hometown

Words and Music by Mary Chapin Carpenter

G
C
— down in the bomb shel - ter,
ap - peared with - out a — trace, and
look - ing back from such a dis - tance, when the
F
C/E
suf - fered through the won - der years — and si -
some of us are still at large, — still search -
road not tak - en dis - ap - pears — in - to
G
C
lence at the din - ner hour. — But once —
ing for a bet - ter place. — But once —
the path of least re - sis - tance. — But once —

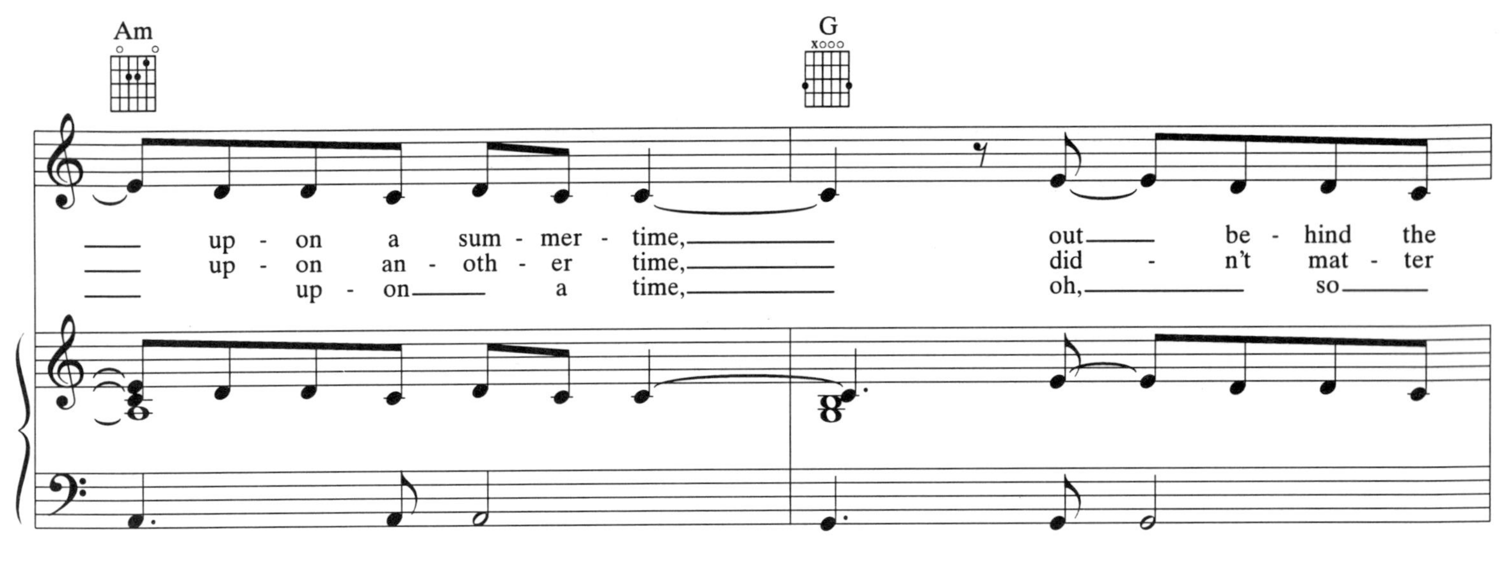
Am
G
up - on a sum - mer - time, out be - hind the
up - on an - oth - er time, did - n't mat - ter
up - on a time, oh, so

F
old ga - rage, we were buzz -
what they said. It did - n't mat -
long a - go, un - der - neath

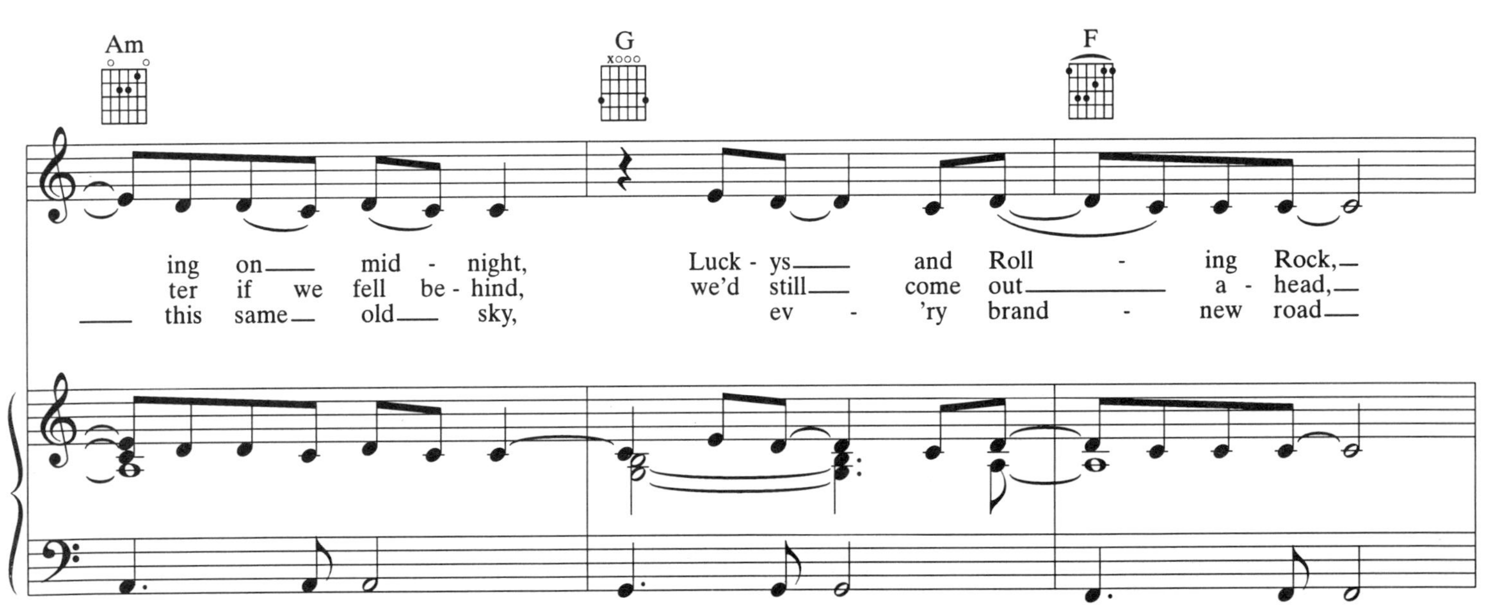
Am
G
F
ing on mid - night, Luck - ys and Roll - ing Rock,
ter if we fell be - hind, we'd still come out a - head,
this same old sky, ev - 'ry brand - new road

G
C
F
G
C
think - ing we were he - roes in our own home - town.
'cause we be - lieved in he - roes in that old home - town.
would know that we were he - roes in our own home - town.
F
G
Am
F
Noth - ing less than he - roes in that old
Hey, you could be a he - ro in your own
Noth - ing less than he - roes in that old
G
C
F
To Coda
1.
G
C
home - town.
home - town.
home - town.
Some mar -

2.
G
C
Am7
Now I'm long a - way and ver - y far from gaz -
G
C
Am7
ing at an eve - ning sky, from wish - ing on a shoot - ing star,
G
C
from think - ing that a heart can't lie. This world
F
Am
is gon - na wear you thin, knot you up and spin you 'round.

F
This world will take its aim, call you ev-'ry name, try-
D/F♯
D7
F
ing to bring you down.
G
Am
F
G
C
F
G
Am
F
G
C
D.S. al Coda
Ev-

Coda
G
C
F
G
C
F
We still loved a he - ro in our own home - town.
G
Am
F
G
C
F
Ba - by, you can be a he - ro in your own home - town.
G
C
F
G
Am
F
G
C
F
G
Am
F
G
C

Naked To The Eye

Words and Music by Mary Chapin Carpenter

A
D/A
E/A
A
streets; been de - cid - ing what's true. Been hands in my
a - part, but they're nev - er far a - way. I can see her in your
D
E
A
pock - ets, coat col - lar up, think - ing 'bout you.
eyes, hear her in your voice, and I have to turn a - way.
D
E
A
D/A
E
I've been talk - ing to my - self, giv - ing fate the third
Oh, what cov - et is to ache, is what ach - ing is

A
D
degree. Been eyes on the pavement, admitting my
to me, for the arms of a man who knows who I
E
A
part to strangers passing me. And I know it isn't
am and where I need to be. And if I know what I
D
E
A
fair, but nothing's ever been.
know, then the lonely can't pretend.
F♯m
E
D
Hey, when you look at me, baby, my god, how I feel so good
Ooh, when you look at me, baby, my god, how I feel so whole

E
To Coda
A
again.
again.
I don't know where I went wrong,
D/A
E/A
A
but it isn't right to lie.
Hey, when you look at me, ba-
F♯m
E
D
E
A
by, my heart's wide open, naked to the eye.
A
N.C.
D/A
E/A

A
D
E
A
D.S. al Coda
D
E
Now, some lov - ers are
Coda
A
D
E
Is there heav - en af - ter all,
or just this emp -
A
F#m
E
ty space
that no a - mount of time nor com - fort in its

D
E
hands can ev - er help me face?
Which is worse is yet
A
D/A
E/A
A
to come, your re - buff or my re - sign?
a spell, un - bro - ken by a sigh.
F♯m
E
D
E
Hey, when you look at me, ba - by, I'm help - less as a child, na - ked to the
Oh, when you look at me, ba - by, I'm go - ing no - where, just na - ked to the
A
1.
D
E
2.
eye. It's like a fev - er and
eye.
Yeah, when you look at me, ba -

F♯m
E
D
E
by, ev - 'ry - thing's there,
na - ked to the
A
eye.
Yeah, when you look at me, ba -
F♯m
E
D
E
by, I have - n't got a prayer,
na - ked to the
A
D
A
eye.

I Can See It Now

Words and Music by Mary Chapin Carpenter

Moderately fast

G

mf

Am7

C

Am7
C
sud - den - ly you're there walk - ing with some - bod - y's else.
It's too late for me to walk the oth - er way.
Some - thing left un - said and the noth - ing left to say.
G
I can see it now, what's right up a - head. A
I can hear it now, ask - ing how I've been.
I can feel it now like weath - er in my bones, be -
Am7
C
scene I've played a thou - sand times o - ver in my head.
Oh, and by the way, have you met my friend?
fore it e - ven comes, be - fore I e - ven know.

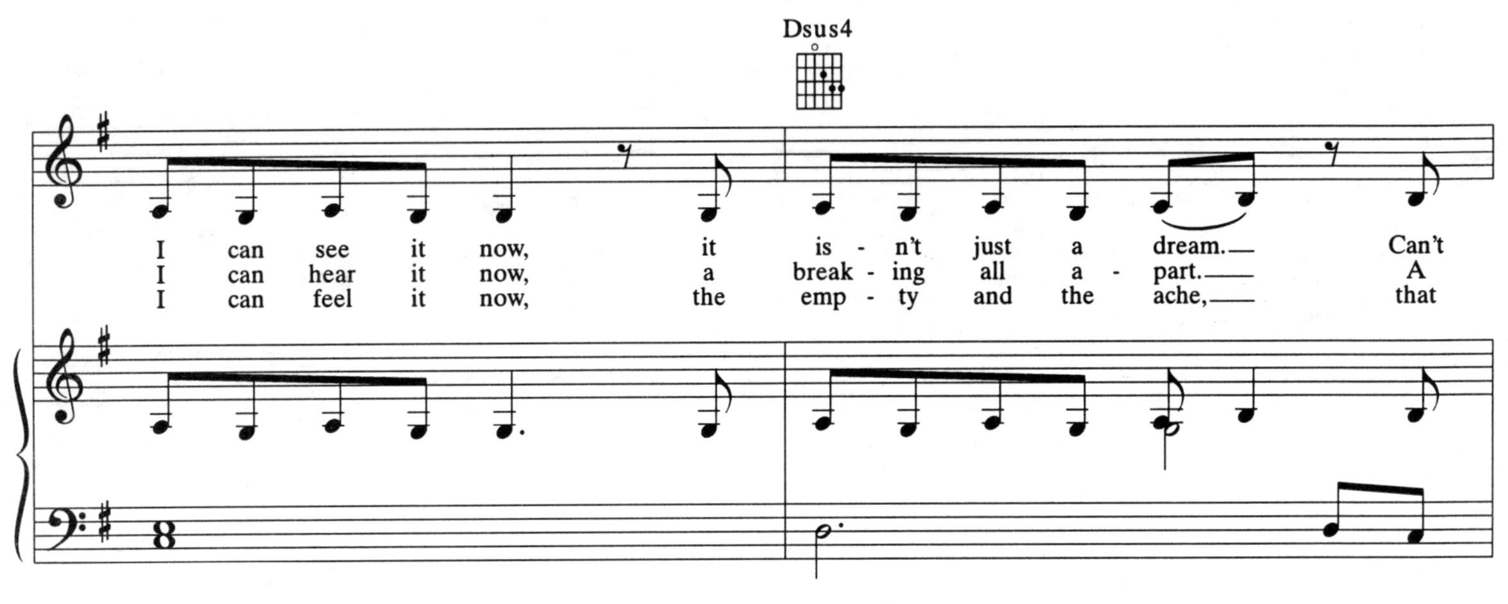

Dsus4
I can see it now, it is - n't just a dream.___ Can't
I can hear it now, a break - ing all a - part.___ A
I can feel it now, the emp - ty and the ache,___ that

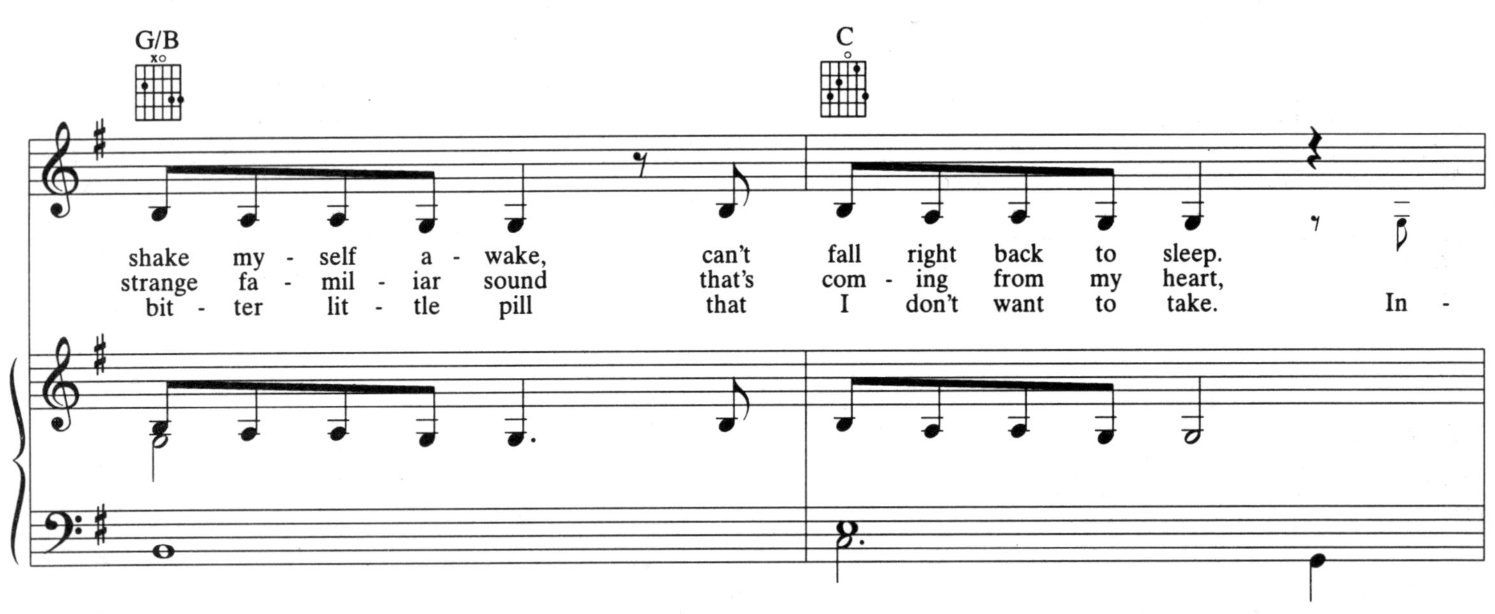

G/B
C
shake my - self a - wake, can't fall right back to sleep.
strange fa - mil - iar sound that's com - ing from my heart,
bit - ter lit - tle pill that I don't want to take. In -

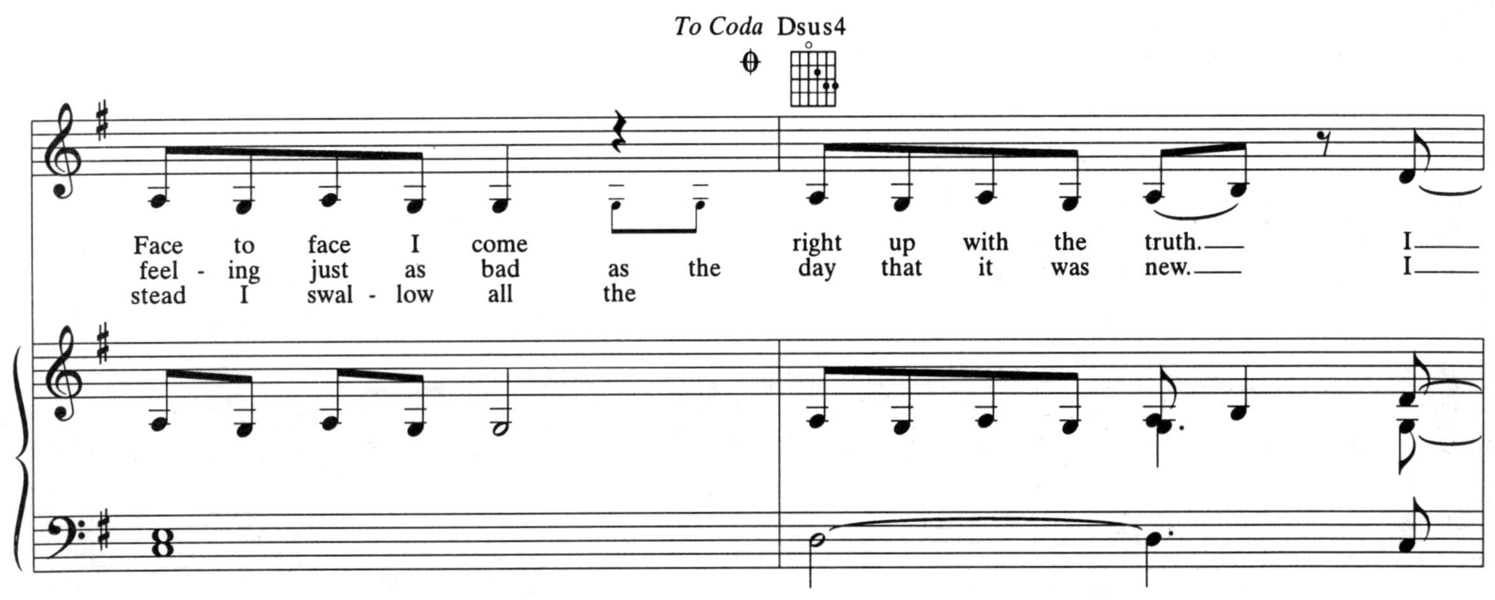

To Coda
Dsus4
Face to face I come right up with the truth.___ I___
feel - ing just as bad as the day that it was new.___ I___
stead I swal - low all the

G/B
1. C
Dsus4
G
can see it now. I'm still not o - ver you.
can see it now. I'm
2. C
Dsus4
G
still not o - ver you.
(Sing 1st time only)
Am7
C
(Sing 1st time only) Oh.
B♭
Am7
G
When you're out of sight, ba - by, you're still on my mind. You're much too hard to lose, you're

B♭
Am7
too eas - y to find, like a bot - tle to a drunk, like trou - ble to a fool. I've
C
Dsus4
D.S. al Coda
on - ly ev - er seen just what I've want - ed to.
Coda
Dsus4
G/B
C
Dsus4
pride I ev - er knew, to crawl back if you asked, all that I would do.
G
Am7
Oh,

C
G
I can see it now.
Am7
C
B♭
Am7
1.2.3.
G
4.
G

I Want To Be Your Girlfriend

Words and Music by Mary Chapin Carpenter

A B E A B E
new love. I want to be the one that you can't
B A E A B
get e - nough of. { I want to be your girl - friend, / I'm gon - na be your girl - friend, }
E A B C♯m G♯m7
4fr. 4fr.
no - bod - y else - 's but yours. I want to be the
A B E To Coda B A
one who you'll do an - y - thing for.

E B A E
Nev - er thought I'd ev - er wind up in a daze
You used to be just this guy I knew from that same
B A E B A
like this. I nev - er thought I'd ev - er find my -
old scene. For all the time that I've known
E B A B
self won - d'ring how you kiss. I see you near - ly
you, just now I'm no - tic - ing that ev - 'ry - thing there

E
F♯
B
ev - 'ry day, and ev - 'ry day I lose my nerve that
is to feel feels worse than an - y teen - age crush. And
E
F♯
I built up the night be - fore, re - hears - ing ev - 'ry
all the times that I've been near you, now I can't get
B
E
A
B
sin - gle word. I want to be your girl - friend.
near e - nough. Oh, I want to be your girl - friend,

1.
2.
E
A
B
C♯m
G♯m7
4fr.
I want to be your new love. I want to be the
no - bod - y else - 's but yours.
one that you can't get e - nough of.
I want to be the one who you'll do an - y - thing for.

A
C°7
I just keep on hop - ing that you're
E/B
gon - na see if I could no - tice you, then
A♯m7♭5
A
you could no - tice me. Then I'd be

B
more to you, oh, I just wan - na be.
E
A
B
E
A
B
C♯m
4fr.
F♯m7
A
G♯m
4fr.
E
B
A
D.S. al Coda
𝄋

Coda
B
A
E
an - y - thing for.
A
B
E
A
B
E
A
B
E
A
E
D
E
D
E
D
E
D
E

CRYSTAL POOL

Complete Lyrics

In Album Order

Keeping The Faith

When it's been that kind of day baby
When everything is not what it should be
Everybody's had their say
Let's just say today is history

Chorus:
And keep keeping the faith
Keeping the faith, everyday
We're keeping the faith
Keep keeping the faith, don't give it away

When your head's not making sense baby
When your heart is just a mystery
When you're sitting on the fence
Instead of knowing where you're supposed to be

Repeat Chorus

All the style, all the money, all the power you can buy
Won't do nothing if there's something missing way down deep inside

It's the weary, it's the lonesome
It's the forest that we just can't see
Don't forget now, there ain't no one
Who isn't trying to see beyond the trees

Repeat Chorus

Keeping the faith
Keeping the faith, everyday
We'll be keeping the faith
Keeping the faith, don't give it away

Hero In Your Own Hometown

e were born during the boom times, played house down in the bomb shelter
Suffered through the wonder years, and silence at the dinner hour
But once upon a summertime, out behind the old garage
We were buzzing on midnight, Luckys and Rolling Rock
Thinking we were heroes in our own hometown
Nothing less than heroes in that old hometown

Some married on a day in June, some disappeared without a trace
And some of us are still at large, still searching for a better place
But once upon another time, it didn't matter what they said
Didn't matter if we fell behind, we'd still come out ahead
'Cause we believed in heroes in that old hometown
Hey, you could be a hero in your own hometown

Now I'm long away and very far, from gazing at an evening sky
From wishing on a shooting star, from thinking that a heart can't lie
This world is gonna wear you thin, knot you up and spin you 'round
This world will take its aim, call you every name,
trying to bring you down

Everything seems so clear when you're looking back from such a distance
When the road not taken disappears into the path of least resistance
But once upon a time oh so long ago
Underneath this same old sky every brand new road

Would know that we were heroes in our own hometown
Nothing less than heroes in that old hometown
We still loved a hero in our own hometown
Baby you could be a hero in your own hometown

I Can See It Now

I can see it now, walking by myself
And suddenly you're there walking with somebody else
I can see it now, what's right up ahead
A scene I've played a thousand times over in my head

I can see it now, it isn't just a dream
Can't shake myself awake, can't fall right back to sleep
Face to face I come right up to the truth
I can see it now, I'm still not over you

I can hear it now, your voice saying my name
It's too late for me to walk the other way
I can hear it now, asking how I've been
Oh and by the way have you met my friend

I can hear it now, a breaking all apart
A strange familiar sound that's coming from my heart
Feeling just as bad as the day that it was new
I can see it now, I'm still not over you

When you're out of sight, baby you're still on my mind
You're much too hard to lose, you're too easy to find
Like a bottle to a drunk, like trouble to a fool
I've only ever seen, just what I've wanted to

I can feel it now, as you walk away
The something left unsaid and the nothing left to say
I can feel it now like weather in my bones
Before it even comes, before I even know

I can feel it now, the empty and the ache
That bitter little pill that I don't want to take
Instead I'd swallow all the pride I ever knew
To crawl back if you asked, all that I would do
I can see it now

I Want To Be Your Girlfriend

I want to be your girlfriend, I want to be your new love
I want to be the one that you can't get enough of
I want to be your girlfriend, nobody else's but yours
I want to be the one who you'll do anything for

Never thought I'd ever wind up in a daze like this
Never thought I'd ever find myself wondering how you kiss
I see you nearly every day, and every day I lose my nerve
That I built up the night before, rehearsing every single word

I want to be your girlfriend, I want to be your new love
I want to be the one that you can't get enough of

You used to be just this guy I knew from that same old scene
For all the time that I've known you, just now I'm noticing
That everything there is to feel, feels worse than any teenage crush
And all the times that I've been near you, now I can't get near enough

Oh, I want to be your girlfriend, nobody else's but yours
I want to be the one who you'll do anything for

I just keep on hoping that you're gonna see
If I could notice you, then you could notice me
Then I'd be more to you, oh, I just wanna be

I want to be your girlfriend, I want to be your new love
I want to be the one that you can't get enough of
I'm gonna be your girlfriend, nobody else's but yours
I want to be the one who you'll do anything for

Let Me Into Your Heart

You're like a cool breeze to a hot spell
You're like a long drink to a dry well
Oh I know by now there's no use thinking
That it's something in that water I've been drinking
'Cause I would not need even one more drop
If you'd just let me into your heart

You're like a blue sky to a grey day
You're like a new try to an old way
Oh I never needed much convincing 'bout that
Something in my life that's been missing
But I think I know where to find that part
If you'd just let me into your heart

I got a past baby, now who doesn't
I won't ask you to think that I wasn't
Who I was back then, yes it's true
But that was when I didn't know you

You're like a sweet sight to these tired eyes
You're like the first light after a long night
Oh I never believed in the hands of fate
But to be with you baby, I believe I'd wait
Till the end of time for a chance to start
If you'd just let me into your heart

You're like a sweet smile to these tired eyes
You're like the last mile on a long ride
Oh I never believed in the arms of fate
But to be in yours darling, I believe I'd wait
'Till the end of time for a chance to start
If you'd just let me into your heart
'Till the end of time, baby I can start
If you'd just let me into your heart

That's Real

I'm not made of stone, I'm not made of glass
I've been alone, every one has
I've learned to forgive what I'm not
I just try to live with what I've got
Maybe I've got what you need

If you need something that not only feels right
Something that's based on a real life
One thing that's worth every page of the deal
Not some old line, or rose-colored dream
Not some other time, you know what I mean
When I tell you that this is all that it seems and that's real

How far can I crawl out on this limb
There's so far to fall and here comes the wind
There's so much to lose, but love doesn't wait
So I'll be a fool who found out too late
But I've been a fool for far lesser things

And I want something that not only feels right
Something that's based on a real life
One thing that's worth every page of the deal
Not some old line, or rose-colored dream
Not some other time, you know what I mean
When I tell you that this is all that it seems, and that's real

Not some old line or rose-colored dream
Not some other time, you know what I mean
When I tell you that I'm, I'm all that I seem, and that's real
And that's real
And that's real
And that's real

What If We Went To Italy

What if we went to Italy
A suitcase of books and one bag a piece for the summer
I don't speak a word of Italian
Except for Campari and soda for two, how much is a lira
Yes, a villa will do and a breeze, in Tuscany please

What if we spent all of our days, improving our minds,
Learning new ways to be lazy
It wouldn't be too much of a strain
Relax after breakfast 'till lunch comes around
Can't wait for dinner, oh, I need to lie down
And refuel, out by the pool

What if the ancients were lazy like us
Too blissed out to paint, to sketch or to sculpt
Just as relaxed as the tower of Pisa
Not ever missing that old Mona Lisa

What if we never got back on the plane
As summer turned colder and then warmer again
Losing all track of the passing of years
'Til it no longer mattered how long we'd been here

What if we went to Italy
Maybe next year, just you and me for the summer
I still can't speak any Italian
But words are replaced under Sienese skies
By nothing so much as a nod, and a sigh, and a wish to be always like this

Ideas Are Like Stars

Today Joseph is sitting alone, with occasional nods to the waitress
She tops off his cup while she's snapping her gum,
Making her rounds on the lunch shift
Counting out coins, he leaves them arranged in neat lines and circles and arcs
She just stares at the tip that spells out her name and ideas are like stars

And yesterday pedaling down 4th Avenue, between the stalls and the bookshops
The sepia tones of a lost afternoon cradled a curio storefront
And inside the air was thick with the past, as the dust settled onto his heart
And here for a moment is every place in the world and ideas are like stars

They fall from the sky, they run round your head
They litter your sleep as they beckon
They'd teach you to fly without wires or thread
They promise if only you'd let them
For the language of longing never had words,
So how did you speak from your heart
Yet here is a box that swears it has heard that ideas are like stars

Tonight Joseph stood out in the yard, as Debussy played from the kitchen
Celestial companions 'till morning's first lark, shone overhead and he listened
And who was that shadow there by the gate, who was that there standing guard
It was only loneliness, and loneliness waits, and ideas are like stars
Ideas are like stars

Naked To The Eye

Been walking these streets, been deciding what's true
Been hands in my pockets, coat collar up, thinking 'bout you
I've been talking to myself, giving fate the third degree
I've been eyes on the pavement admitting my part to strangers passing me
And I know it isn't fair, but nothing's ever been
Hey when you look at me baby, my god how I feel so good again
I don't know where I went wrong, but it isn't right to lie
Hey when you look at me baby, my heart's wide open, naked to the eye

Now some lovers are apart, but they're never far away
I can see her in your eyes, hear her in your voice and I have to turn away
Oh what covet is to ache, is what aching is to me
For the arms of a man who knows who I am and where I need to be
And if I know what I know, then the lonely can't pretend
When you look at me baby, my god how I feel so whole again
Is there heaven after all, or just this empty space
That no amount of time, nor comfort in its hands can ever help me face
Which is worse is yet to come, your rebuff or my resign
Hey when you look at me baby, I'm helpless as a child, naked to the eye

It's like a fever and a spell, unbroken by a sigh
Oh when you look at me baby I'm going nowhere, just naked to the eye
Yeah when you look at me baby, everything's there, naked to the eye
Hey when you look at me baby, I haven't got a prayer, naked to the eye

The Better To Dream Of You

Every heart has got a story
About love holding out a lure
Baby, when you've been that lonely
You just want a cure

Fool you once, you are forgiven
Fool you twice, you're just a fool
You fear the future's all been written
By the past, and what didn't last

Chorus:
All the better to dream of you
The better to be this side of heaven
Believing again when a dream comes true
The better to dream of you

Every story's got a chapter
That chapter will be defined
By what's before and what comes after
This one is mine
Everything that came before us
Wore me out and weighed me down
You raised me up like a gospel chorus
Rock steady on solid ground

Repeat Chorus

Like an old-time tent revival, I felt my heart come back alive
No preacher baby, no Bible, just this love to testify

Repeat Chorus (3 times)

Sudden Gift Of Fate

Some people need to know what to expect
Need to keep control, need to keep one step ahead of every chance,
As if chance decides
who it's gonna pass, who it will reward
They don't understand, chances don't keep score
They just find us when we're there to find

And so this has to be, a sudden gift of fate
You're nothing less to me than a sudden gift of fate
It's not as if it comes down to your turn that someone
Somewhere feels you've earned
You just learn to wait for sudden gifts of fate

Some people have never been the lonely kind
Never called a friend in the middle of the night
Just to hear a voice say it's okay
And now I hear you speak each and every word
That I didn't think lonely people heard
You took a long night and turned it into day

And so this has to be, a sudden gift of fate
You're nothing less to me than a sudden gift of fate
It's not as if it comes down to your turn that someone
Somewhere feels you've earned
You just learn to wait for sudden gifts of fate

You can celebrate, gifts are never late
You just learn to wait for sudden gifts of fate

A Place In The World

What I'm looking for, after all this time
Keeps me moving forward, trying to find it
Since I learned to walk all I've done is run
Ready, on my mark, doesn't everyone
Need a place in the world

Could be right before your very eyes
Just beyond a door that's open wide
Could be far away or in your own backyard
There are those who say, you can look too hard
For your place in the world

Takes some of us a little longer
A few false starts gonna make you stronger
When I'm sure I've finally found it
Gonna wrap these arms all around it

Could be one more mile, or just one step back
In a lover's smile, down a darkened path
Friends will take our side, enemies will curse us
But to be alive is to know your purpose
It's your place in the world
Your place in the world
Your place in the world

Let Me Into Your Heart

Words and Music by Mary Chapin Carpenter

C
F
C
C7
long drink to a dry well. Oh, I
new try to an old way. Oh, I
first light af - ter a long night. Oh, I
F
know by now there's no use think - ing that it's
nev - er need - ed much con - vinc - ing 'bout that
nev - er be - lieved in the hands of fate, but to
C
F
C
some - thing in that wa - ter I've been drink - ing, 'cause I
some - thing in my life that's been miss - ing. But I
be with you, ba - by, I be - lieve I'd wait till the

G
would not need e - ven one more drop if you'd
think I know where to find that part if you'd
end of time for a chance to start if you'd
C F
1.
C G
just let me in - to your heart. You're like a
just let me in - to your heart.
just let me in - to your heart.
2.
C F C
I got a past, babe. Now, who does - n't? I won't
Instrumental...

F
C
Am
ask you to think that I was-n't who I was back then.
D7
To Coda
G
D.S. (take 2nd ending) al Coda
Yes, it's true, but that was when I, I did-n't know you. You're like a
Coda
G
C
F
C
F
You're like a sweet smile to these tired eyes. You're like the

C F C C7 F
last mile on a long ride. Oh, I never believed in the
F♯° C/G Am
arms of fate, but to be in yours, darlin', I believe I'd wait till the
G C F
end of time for a chance to start if you'd just let me into your heart.

C
G
Till the end of time, baby, I can start if you'd
C
F
C
F
just let me in - to your heart.
C
F
C
F
C
F
C
F
C
F
C

What If We Went To Italy

Words and Music by Mary Chapin Carpenter

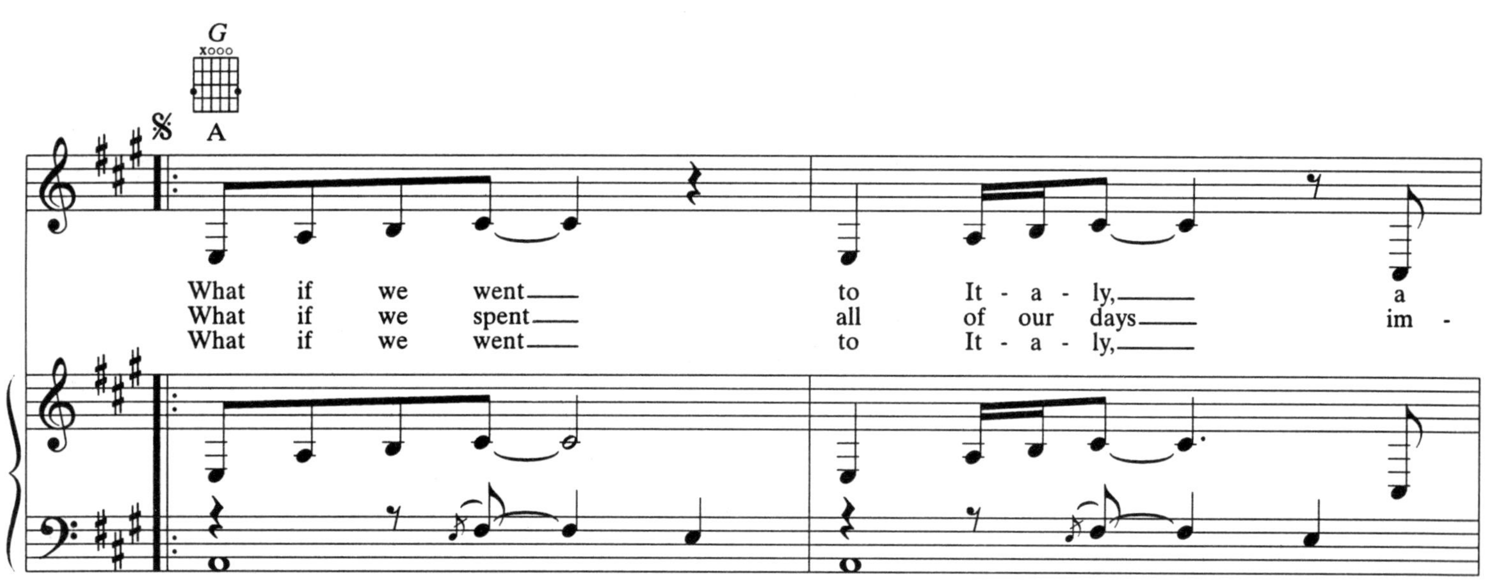

C
D
sum - mer? I don't speak a word of I - tal -
la - zy? It would - n't be too much of a
sum - mer? I still can't speak an - y I - tal -
G
A
ian, ex -
strain. Re -
ian, but
D
E
cept for "Cam - par - i and so - da for two," "How
lax af - ter break - fast till lunch comes a - round.
words are re - placed un - der Si - e - nese skies by

To Coda
much is a li - re?," "Yes, a vil - la will do,
Can't wait for din - ner, oh, I need to lie down
noth - ing so much as a
C
D
and a breeze in Tus - ca - ny, please."-
and re - fuel out by the pool.
G
A
1.
2.

C D Bm
D E C♯m
What if the an - cients were la - zy like us, too blissed out to paint, to
Em Am B7
F♯m Bm C♯7
sketch, or to sculpt, just as re - laxed as the Tow - er of Pi - sa,
Em G7 C
F♯m A7 D
not ev - er miss - ing that old Mo - na Li - sa. What if we nev - er got back
D Bm
E C♯m
on the plane, as sum - mer turned cold - er and then

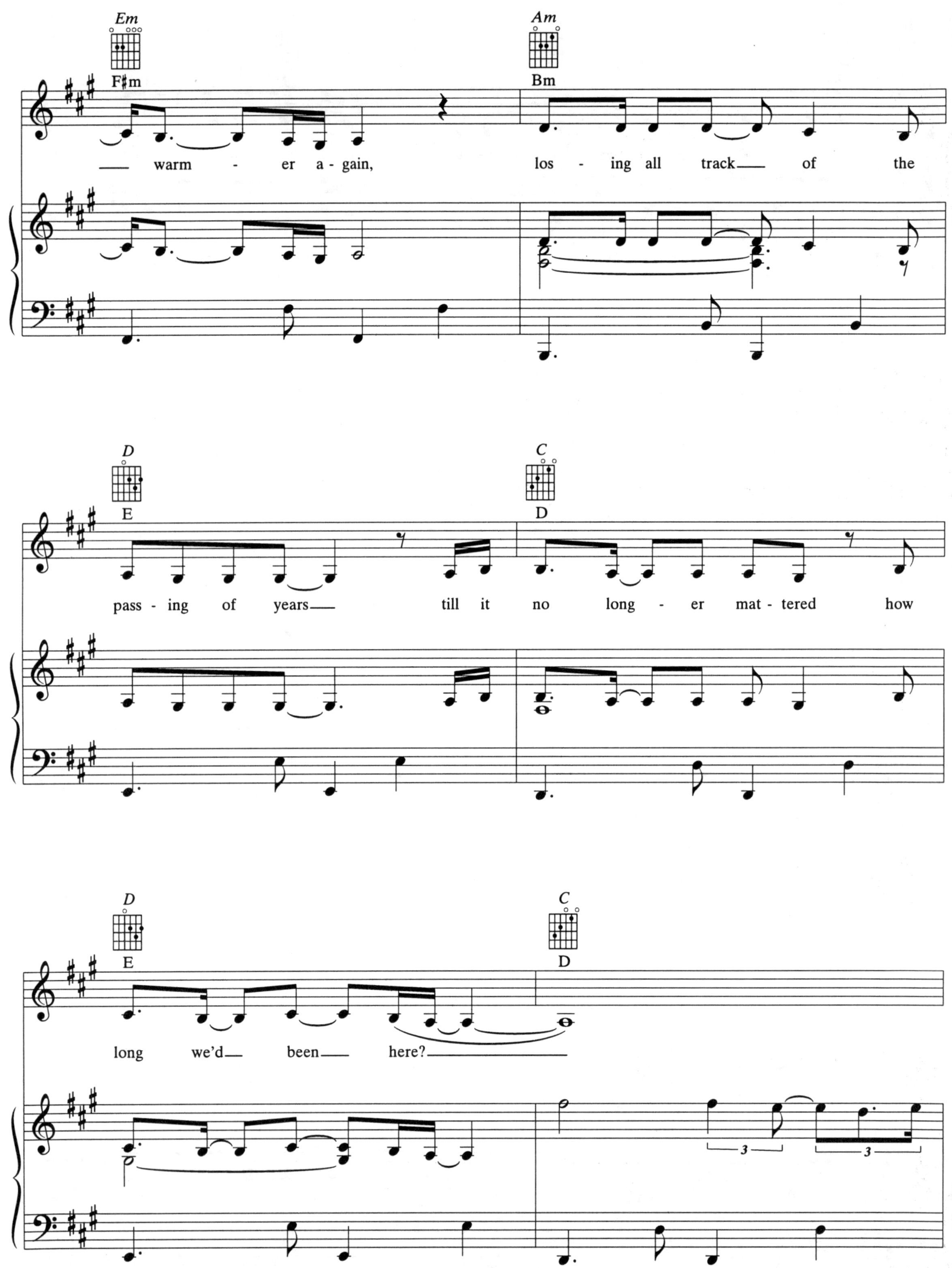
Em
F♯m
warm - er a - gain,
Am
Bm
los - ing all track of the
D
E
pass - ing of years till it
C
D
no long - er mat - tered how
D
E
long we'd been here?
C
D

D
E
Bm
C♯m
Em
F♯m
Am
Bm
B7
C♯7
C
D
D
E
D.S. al Coda
Coda
C
D
nod and a sigh, and a wish
Bm
C♯m
Am
Bm
G
A
to be al - ways like this.
rit.

Ideas Are Like Stars

Words and Music by Mary Chapin Carpenter

Fsus2
(T)
Asus2
G
B
C/E
E/G♯
mak - ing her rounds_ on the lunch shift. And
cra - dled cu - ri - o store - front. And
shone o - ver - head_ and he lis - tened. And
Fsus2
(T)
Asus2
G
B
C/E
E/G♯
count - ing out coins, he leaves them ar - ranged_ in
in - side, the air was thick with the past,_ as the
who was that shad - ow there by the gate?_
Fsus2
(T)
Asus2
G
B
C/E
E/G♯
neat lines_ and cir - cles_ and arcs._ She just
dust set - tled on - to_ his heart,_ as
Who was_ that there stand - ing guard?_ It was

Fsus2
(T)
Asus2
G
B
C/E
E/G♯
stares at the tip that spells out her name, and
here for a moment is ev-'ry place in the world, and
on-ly lone-li-ness and lone-li-ness waits, and
To Coda
1.
i-deas are like stars.
i-deas are like
i-deas are like
And yes-

2.
G
C/E
Fsus2
C
G
C
B
E/G♯
Asus2
E
B
E
stars. They fall from the sky; they run 'round your head; they
Fsus2
C
G
C
Fsus2
C
Asus2
E
B
E
Asus2
E
lit-ter your sleep as they beck-on. They'd teach you to fly with-out
G
C
Fsus2
C
G
B
E
Asus2
E
B
wi-res or thread; they'd prom-ise if on-ly you'd let them. For the lan-
C/E
Fsus2
G
C/E
Fsus2
E/G♯
Asus2
B
E/G♯
Asus2
guage of long-ing nev-er had words, so how did you speak

G
C/E
Fsus2
G
C/E
B
E/G♯
Asus2
B
E/G♯
from your heart?
Yet here is a box that swears it has heard
Fsus2
G
C/E
Fsus2
C
Asus2
B
E/G♯
Asus2
E
that ideas are like stars.
G
C
Fsus2
C
G
Fsus2
C
B
E
Asus2
E
B
Asus2
E
G
C
Fsus2
C
G
D.C. al Coda
B
E
Asus2
E
B

Coda
G
B
C/E
E/G♯
Fsus2
(T)
Asus2
stars.
I - deas
G
B
C/E
E/G♯
Fsus2
(T)
Asus2
C
E
G
B
C
E
are like stars.
Fsus2
(T)
Asus2
C
E
G
B
Fsus2
(T)
Asus2
C
E
G
B
C
E
Fsus2
(T)
Asus2
C
E
G
B
C
E
rit.

Sudden Gift Of Fate

Words and Music by Mary Chapin Carpenter

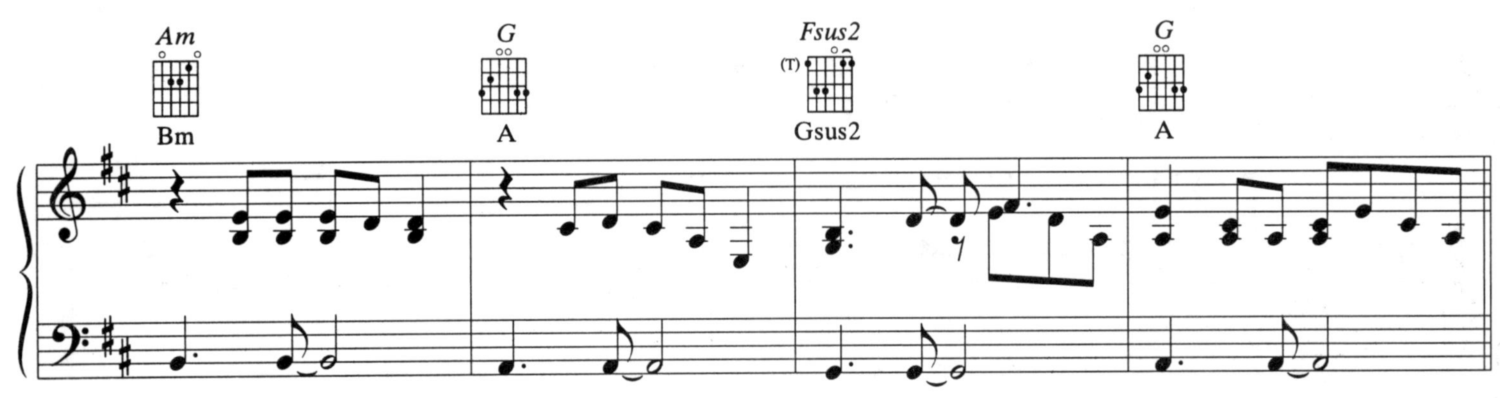

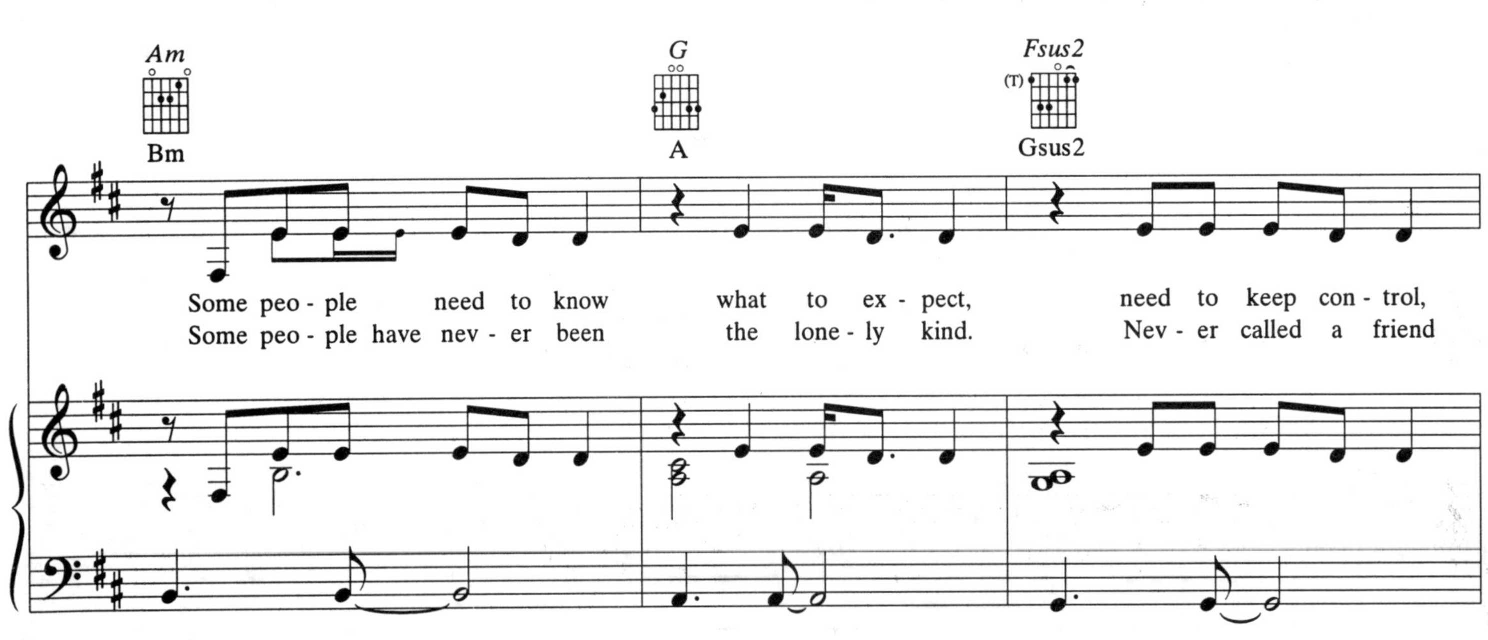

G
Am
G
A
Bm
A
need to keep one step a - head of ev - 'ry chance, as if chance de -
in the mid - dle of the night, just to hear a voice say it's o -
Fsus2
G
Am
Gsus2
A
Bm
cides
kay.
who it's gon - na pass,
And now I hear you speak
G
Fsus2
G
A
Gsus2
A
who it will re - ward. They don't un - der - stand; chanc - es don't keep score.
each and ev - 'ry word that I did - n't think lone - ly peo - ple heard.

Am
G
Fsus2
(T)
Bm
A
Gsus2
They just find us when we're there to find.
You took a long night and turned it in - to day.
G
C
Em
A
D
F♯m
And so, this has to be a sud - den gift of
Fsus2
(T)
G
C
Gsus2
A
D
fate.
You're noth - ing less to me

Em Fsus2 G
F♯m Gsus2 A
than a sud - den gift of fate. It's not as
Fsus2 G Am
Gsus2 A Bm
if it comes down to your turn that some - one, some - where
Dm C/E Fsus2 G Fsus2 G
Em D/F♯ Gsus2 A Gsus2 A
feels you've earned. You just learn to wait for
1. 2.
Fsus2 G Fsus2 G Fsus2 G
Gsus2 A Gsus2 A Gsus2 A
sud - den gifts of fate. You can

Fsus2
G
Gsus2
A
Fsus2/A
G/B
Gsus2/B
A/C♯
(T)
cel - e - brate.
Gifts are nev - er late.
You just learn to wait for
sud - den gifts of fate.
Repeat and fade

That's Real

Words and Music by Mary Chapin Carpenter

C
Dm
Am
I've been a - lone, ev - 'ry - one
There's so far to fall and here comes the
Bb
C
Bb
has.
wind.
I've learned to for -
There's so much to
Am
Bb
Am
give what I'm not. I just try to live with what I've
lose, but love does - n't wait. So I'll be a fool who found out too

B♭
Am
got.
And may - be I've
got
what you
late.
But I've been a fool for
far less - er
B♭
C
F
need.
If you need
things.
And I want
some - thing
that
F/A
B♭sus2
C
not on - ly feels right,
some - thing that's based on a real life.
F
F/A
B♭
One thing that's worth ev - 'ry page of the deal.

C
B♭
Am
Not some old line, or rose-colored
dream. Not some other time, you know what I mean
when I tell you that
when I tell you that
To Coda
Dm
this is all that it seems, and that's real.
I'm, I'm all that I

Dm
Am
1.
B♭
C
2.
B♭
C
D.S. al Coda
Coda
B♭
F
C/E
Dm
seem,
and that's
real,
Am
B♭
1.
C
and that's
real.
And that's

2.
C
F
F/A
B♭
C
F
F/A
B♭
C
Dm

The Better To Dream Of You

Words and Music by Mary Chapin Carpenter

*Recorded a half step lower.

F/A
G
F/A
you just a want a cure.
This one is mine.
Fool you once, you are
Ev - 'ry - thing that came
G
F/A
G/B
for - giv - en.
be - fore us
Fool you twice, you're just a fool.
wore me out and weighed me down.
C/E
F
G
Am
F
You fear the fu - ture's all been writ - ten
You raised me up like a gos - pel cho - rus.
by the past, and what
Rock stead - y on
G
C
F
G
did - n't last. All the
sol - id ground. The
bet - ter to dream of you.
The

C
F
G
C
F
bet - ter to be this side of heav - en. Be - liev - ing a - gain when a dream comes true.
some - dreams come true.
G
Am
F
G
1.
F
The bet - ter to dream of you.
G
2.
B♭
you.
3
F/A
G7sus4
Like an old - time tent re - viv - al, I felt my heart come back

C
F/A
a - live.
No preach - er, ba - by, no Bi - ble,
Am
G
C
F
just this love to tes - ti - fy.
G
C
F
G
C
F
G
Am
F
G
Oh, the

C F G C F
bet - ter to dream of you. The bet - ter to be this
Bet - ter to dream of you. Yeah, strang - er things, they
Bet - ter to dream of you. The bet - ter to be this
you.
Instrumental (till end)
G C F
side of heav - en. Be - liev - ing a - gain some
might have hap - pened. Be - liev - ing a - gain that
side of heav - en. Be - liev - ing a - gain some
1.2.
3.
D.S. and fade
G Am F G F G
dreams come true. The bet - ter to dream of... bet - ter to dream of
dreams come true. The bet - ter to dream of...
dreams come true. The

A Place In The World

Words and Music by Mary Chapin Carpenter

F
C
B♭
keeps me mov - ing for - ward, try - ing to find it.
just be - yond a door that's o - pen wide.
in a lov - er's smile, down a dark - ened path.
F
C
B♭
Since I learned to walk, all I've done is run.
Could be far a - way, or in your own back - yard.
Friends will take our side, en - e - mies will curse us.
To Coda
1.
F
C
B♭
Read - y, on my mark. Does - n't ev - 'ry - one
There are those who say
But to be a - live

C
F
B♭
C
F
need a place in the world?
B♭
2. C
B♭
C
F/A
you can look too hard
B♭
C
F/A
B♭
for your place in the world.
C
B♭
C
Takes some of us a lit - tle long - er. A few false

B♭
F
C
starts gon - na make you strong - er. And when I'm sure
B♭
F/A
Gm7
3fr.
I've fi - n'lly found it, gon - na wrap these arms
C
F
all a - round it.
C
B♭
F
C
B♭
F

C
B♭
F
C
B♭
C
B♭
C
B♭
F
C
B♭
F
Gm7
3fr.
C
D.S. al Coda
Coda
C
B♭
C
F/A
B♭
is to know your pur - pose.
It's your place in the world.
C
F/A
B♭
C
F
Your place in the world.

B♭
C
F
B♭
Your place in the world.
C
F
B♭
C
F
B♭
C
F
B♭
1. C
F
B♭
2. C
F

Cherry Lane Music

"Quality In Printed Music"